to

from

For my beautiful Flora, our little sunbeam x

Published by **Lion Children's Books**
www.lionhudson.com
Part of the SPCK Group
SPCK, 36 Causton Street, London, SW1P 4ST

ISBN 978 0 7459 7885 7
First edition 2022

A catalogue record for this book is available from the British Library

Printed and bound in China, February 2022, LH54

Special BIBLE Stories

Antonia Woodward

LION
CHILDREN'S

Contents

Adam and Eve and the Fascinating Fruit

First, there was nothing.

Then, God said, "Let's have some…

LIGHT!"

And brightness shone *all* around.

"Now we can see, let's fill the place with colour!"

And with these words, the skies blazed blue and the seas sparkled green. Trees and flowers popped up like splashes of paint.

9

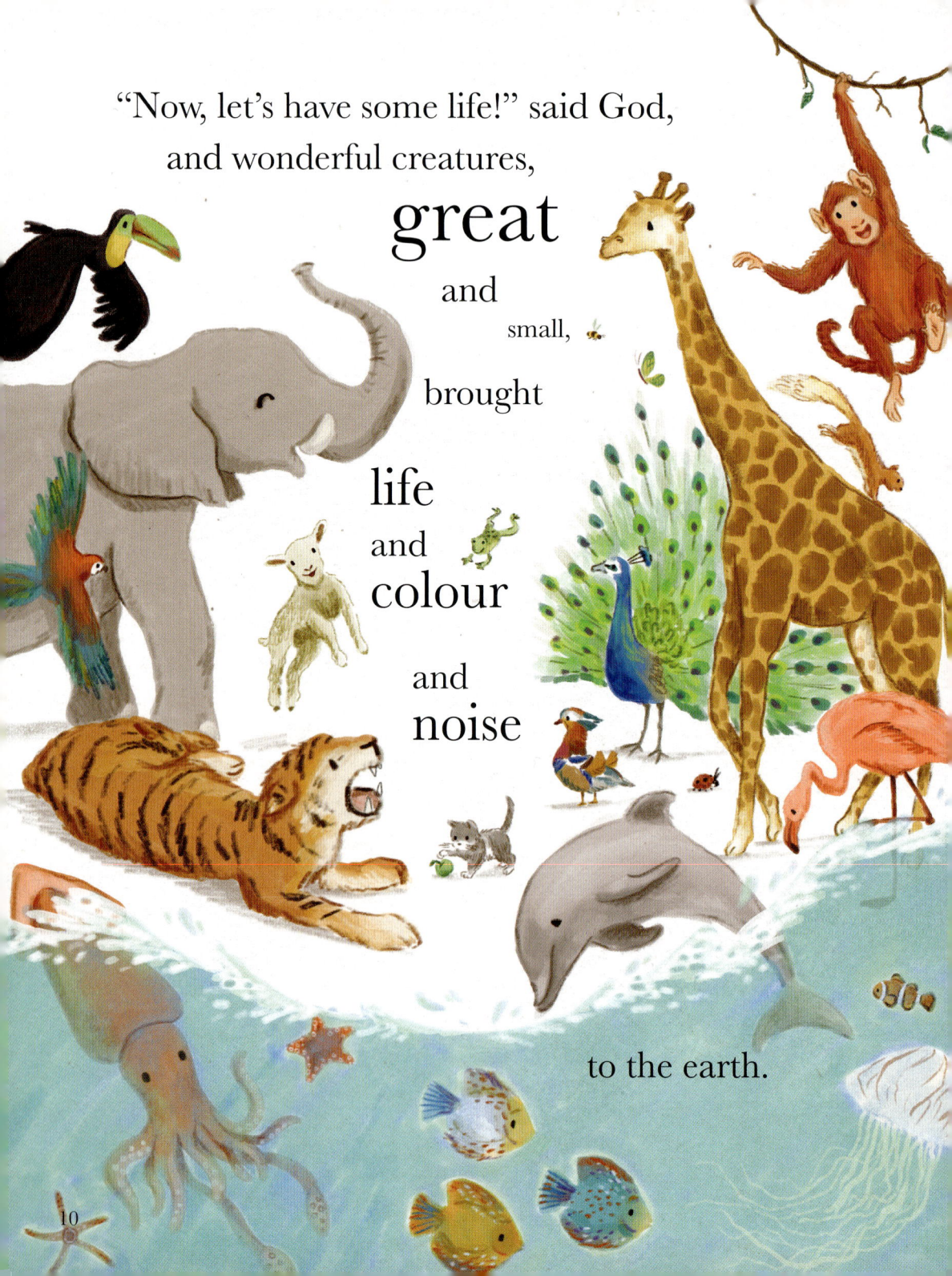

"Now, let's have some life!" said God,
and wonderful creatures,

great

and

small,

brought

life

and

colour

and

noise

to the earth.

"And finally, I have saved the best until last," said God. He carefully made two people, a man named Adam and a woman named Eve, and he put them in his Special Garden.

The whole earth was beautiful beyond words, perfect in every way.

Then God said to Adam and Eve, "I'm giving you a gift – my beautiful earth and everything in it is now yours to enjoy!

I keep only one thing for myself: the tree in the middle of the garden, which is called the 'Tree of the Knowing of Good and Bad'.

Do not eat the fruit of that tree.

But everything else is yours."

One day, Adam and Eve met a sly animal.
"Have you seen how lovely the Tree of Knowing looks today?" it hissed.

"Oh, it's very lovely," agreed Eve. "That's the tree that God looks after. Its fruit is the only food in the garden that we're not allowed to eat."

And the snake replied,
"Have you seen how the fruit
glows in the evening
sun?"

Every day, the snake would slide up to
Eve and ask a question.

"Doesn't the
fruit
look
beautiful?

Doesn't it
smell
delicious?"

Until one day it asked...

"I wonder how it

tastes?"

Eve looked up at the tree.

"If I just take one, nobody will notice," she thought.

She reached up, plucked a little fruit, and took a bite. It was *heavenly*.

She gave it to Adam.

"We won't have any more after this," said Adam. And he took a bite.

And then Adam and Eve knew why it was called
The Tree of the Knowing of Good and Bad.

Before, they had only known what it was to be Good.
Now, they knew what it was to feel Bad. And they
didn't like it one bit.

Just then, God called to them, "Adam? Eve?"
"Eve gave me the fruit to eat!" said Adam.
"The snake told me to eat it!" said Eve.

God was
SO
disappointed.

"Every good thing on earth was yours,
but you took the

one fruit I asked

you

not

to.

When you ate that fruit, you let Bad into the world.
It makes me sad but you won't be able to live in my
Special Garden anymore."

"Oh, **please** don't make us **leave!**" Adam and Eve cried.

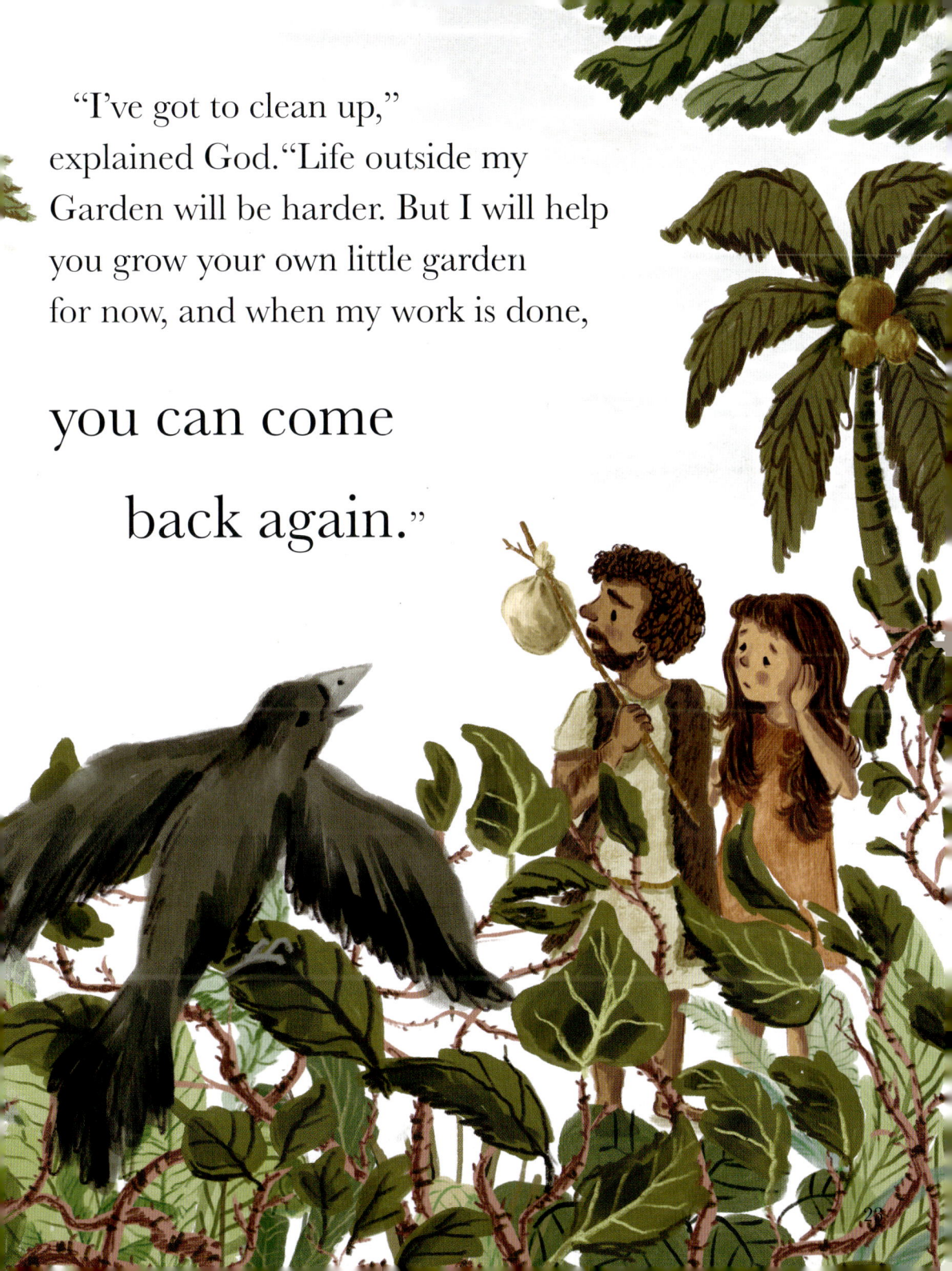

"I've got to clean up,"
explained God. "Life outside my
Garden will be harder. But I will help
you grow your own little garden
for now, and when my work is done,

you can come

back again."

Noah and the Great Big Boat

When God made the earth it was a **good** place

full of love,

and beauty,

and hope.

But somehow, over time, it had
become a **bad** place,
a tangled mess of hate, anger, and selfishness.

God looked down from heaven and saw what a sad place the earth had become.

"It's time for a fresh start," he said.

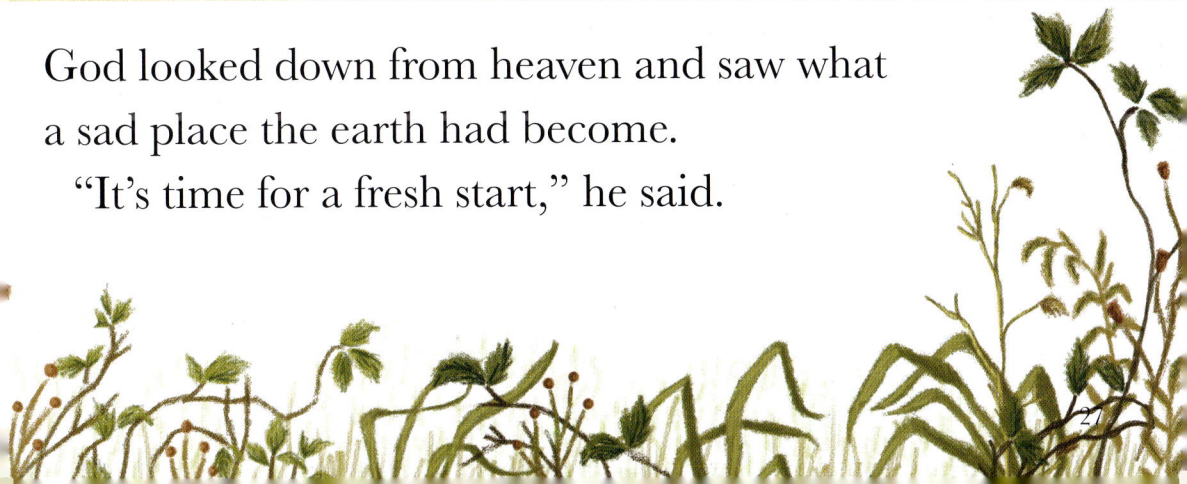

Now, Noah was a good man.
He was kind and peaceful, and
he loved God.

God called to him, "Noah, I need your help!
I'm going to wash the earth clean, and I'd like
you to take care of all the animals while I do."

"But however
will I
find
them all?"
asked Noah.

"Don't worry, I'll bring them all to you," said God.
"But first…

...I want you to build a Great Big Boat."
So, Noah and his family set to work.

They hammered,

and they nailed,

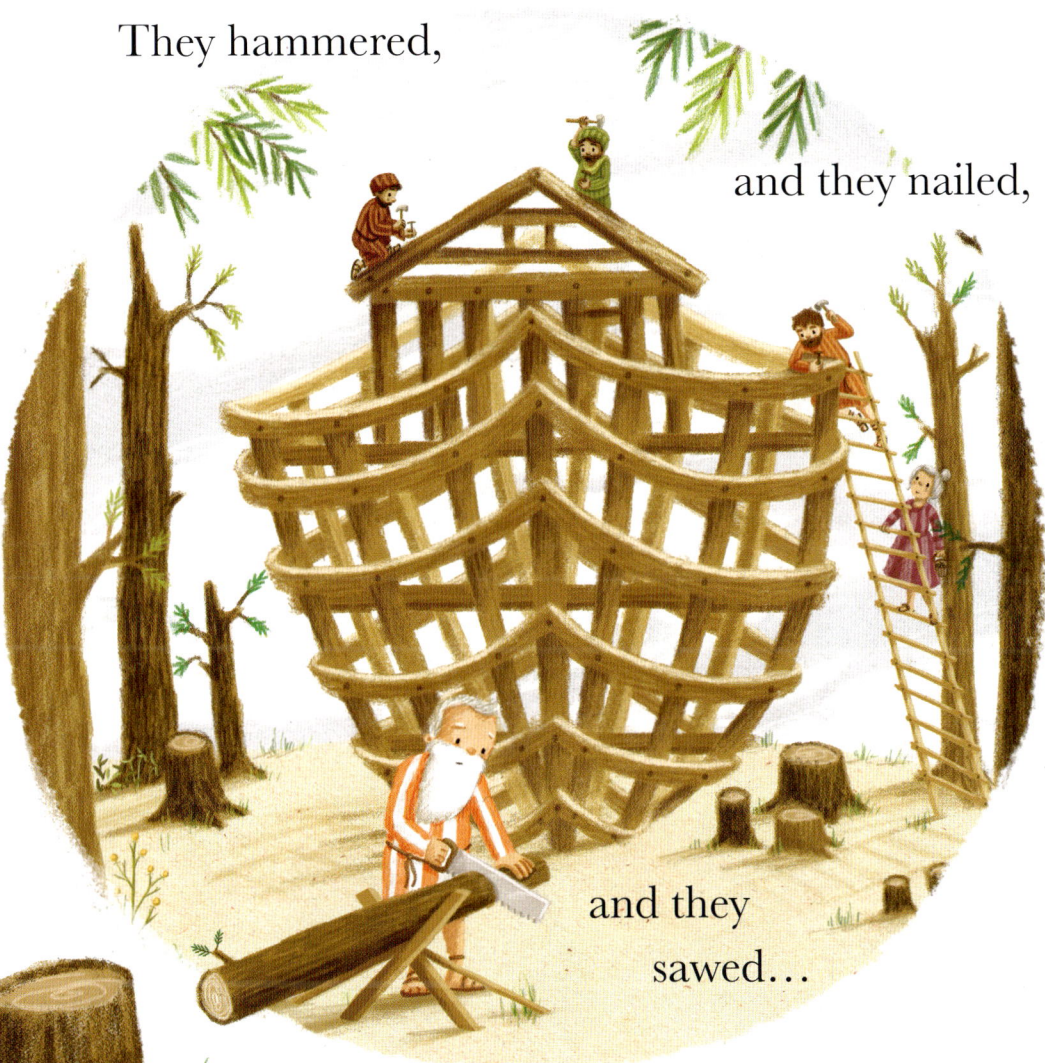

and they
sawed...

...until the boat was complete.
And the very day it was finished...

...STAMPEDE!

From the **spottiest** to the stripiest, the *fastest*

to the s l o w e s t,

the TALLEST

down to the

very, very smallest…

...two of every animal on the earth
flocked to Noah and his Great Big Boat.

Safely inside, the door slammed shut,
the clouds gathered…

…and it began to rain.

And rain…

…and *rain.*

Until eventually –

– the *whole* earth was covered in blue.

For forty days and forty nights it did not stop.

The Great Big Boat and all inside floated on.
Then one delightful day…

... there was

no
more
rain!

With great excitement Noah, let loose a dove. It flew away, but soon came back. There was nowhere for it to land. Noah and the animals waited seven days as the waters went down, and down, and down. Then once again, Noah released the dove.

This time, the dove returned with a fresh green leaf.
"Now, if there is a leaf," said Noah
thoughtfully, "then there is a tree…

and if
there is a
tree,
then there is
dry land
for the tree
to stand on.

Our floating is nearly over!"

God sent a strong wind to dry up
all the floodwater.

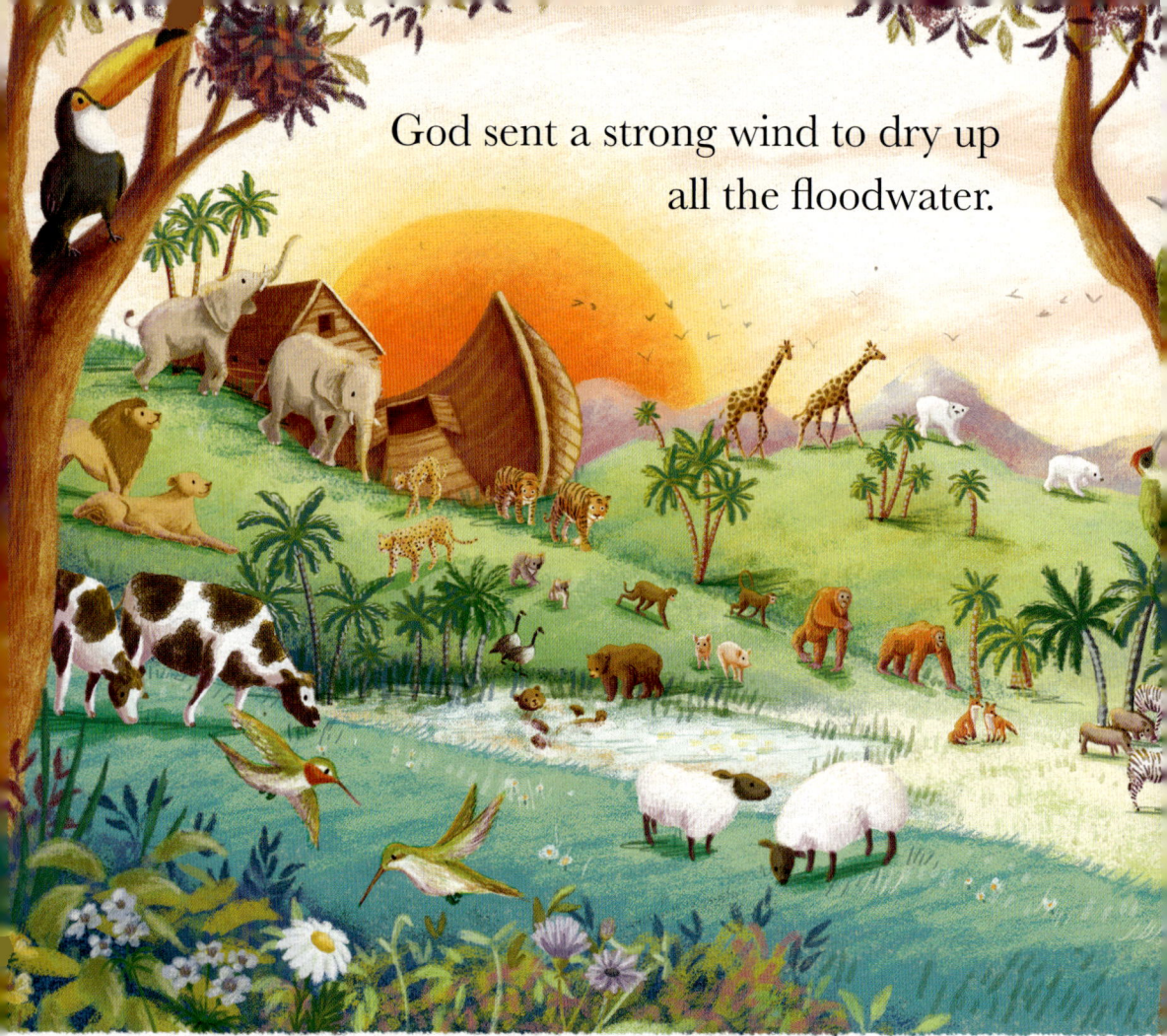

When every last drop had dried up, Noah,
his family, and all the animals stepped down
onto a fresh,

clean,

new

earth.

And God said to them, "This is a new day! Enjoy the land, settle down, make yourselves at home. I will *never* cover the earth with water like this again. Never EVER. When you see a rainbow high up in the clouds, remember this as a sign of my true promise."

And life began again.

The Baby in the Basket

A long time ago, there was a family of Israelites, who were God's people. The pharaoh king of Egypt invited them to leave their homeland to live in his country.

After arriving in Egypt, the family settled down, made new homes, and had children.

Their children had children. And *their* children had children…

Years passed and the family grew bigger and bigger. There were now almost as many Israelites in Egypt as there were Egyptians.

The new pharaoh king
didn't like the Israelites.

They were
different
and he didn't
understand
them.

And because
he didn't
understand
them,
he decided
he didn't
like
them.

Pharaoh wanted the Israelite families to stop getting bigger and bigger, so he made a rule: All Israelite baby girls could stay,

but

any Israelite baby *boys* would be taken away.

In one Israelite family, a lovely new baby boy was born. His family kept him secret for three months, but he became harder and harder

to hide!

It was
time
for a
plan.

45

The family made a basket boat, wrapped the baby boy in a blanket, and made sure he was snug.

"Please look after our baby," the whole family prayed to God. "Please find a home for him and keep him safe."

They placed the basket among the reeds at the edge of the river. The baby's big sister hid and watched to see what would happen.

When a princess came down to the river to bathe, she heard an unexpected noise – the sound of a baby crying! Looking around, she saw the basket floating among the reeds.

"It looks like a little Israelite baby!" she cried.

The baby's sister had a clever idea. She stepped out from among the reeds and asked,

"Would you like me to find an Israelite to look after the baby?"

The princess agreed, and so the girl ran to get her mother.

"Look after this beautiful baby and I will pay for his care," said the princess. She didn't know that this was the baby's real mother. "When he grows up, he can live in the palace with me."

The family were delighted to have their baby back!
"You are so wonderful, God!" they said. "Thank you
for bringing our baby back home."

They cared for him until he
grew a little older, and then
brought him to the palace.
The princess adopted the baby
as her son and named him Moses.

And so the little Israelite baby, Moses, grew up as a prince in Pharaoh's palace.

And while he dressed

and spoke

and ate

like an Egyptian,

inside he knew that really he was an Israelite.
One of God's people.

God had a plan for Moses. He had brought him back home when he was a baby. And one day, he would use him to help the Israelite people return to their homeland, too.

Jonah's Extraordinary Journey

The city of Nineveh was Big. And the city of Nineveh was Bad. Why was it so bad? Because it was full of the

Biggest,

Baddest

Bullies around.

"Enough is enough," decided God. "It's time for a big change."

In a nearby town lived Jonah.
God called to him,

"Jonah!

Go and tell the people of Nineveh that they must start being good, or else their Big Bad city will come tumbling down.

I'm giving them
one more chance."

That was the last thing Jonah wanted to do.

The Ninevites are a bunch of **Big Bad Bullies,** Jonah thought. God shouldn't give *them* another chance!

And he ran down to the shore and jumped on the first boat going in the other direction.

The boat hadn't gone very far before God sent
a strong wind to whip up the waves. The desperate
sailors struggled to keep the boat afloat.

"This is all my fault," said Jonah. "If I had just done what God asked, the boat wouldn't be sinking. Without me, you will all be safe! Oh, help me God!"

And he jumped over the side with a great *splash*.

The waves swirled about Jonah, and he thought this was the end. Then out of the deep blue, a large shadow **loomed**...

Blinking in the darkness, Jonah realized he was in the belly of an enormous fish!

"Oh God," prayed Jonah, "Thank you for rescuing me. I thought I was finished, but you gave me **one more chance!**"

For three days and three nights the fish swam on with Jonah inside.

Then on the fourth morning...

This time, Jonah marched purposefully into the city of Nineveh and told the people God's message.

"You've been such Big Bad Bullies for so long that you've forgotten how to be good! If you don't make big changes, everything you know will come tumbling down.

God is giving you
one more chance –
start being good
and you and your city will be saved!"

All across the city people stopped what they were doing and listened to Jonah.

"This is
terrible!"
they said to each other.

"We will change:
we shall be good from now on."

"Thank you,
GOD,
for giving us

one

more

chance!"

And the people started being good, just as they said they would. And God saved their city.

The Extra Special Baby

A long time ago, a long way away, some very clever men were doing very clever things.

They read lots of scrolls and studied the stars and discovered

A VERY EXCITING PROMISE

written across time.

Someone was coming. Someone new.
Someone so **Extra Special**
that life on earth would
change for ever.

The very clever men packed their bags
and rode off.

"Follow that star!" was their excited cry.

Mary was having a very ordinary day. Ordinary, but happy – Mary was going to marry Joseph.

She was dreaming about all the excitement that lay ahead, when, out of nowhere, a voice called,

"Mary!"

It was an angel.

"I'm here to bring you wonderful news from God. You are going to have a baby!"

"But how can I have a baby?" said Mary, confused. "I'm not married yet."

"Your baby will be extra special because he will be God's own son, come from heaven to live on earth. He will not only be special to you and your family, but to **all** people, everywhere."

Mary thought a while. "If this is what God wants, then I want it too," she said.

Joseph had heard about Mary's baby. He was a little worried and confused.

That night, he had a very bright dream. An angel said to him,

"Don't be worried, Joseph. Take care of Mary because her baby is an

Extra Special Baby.

He is the Son of God. When he is born, name him Jesus, which means 'God saves'."

Now, all the people had
been told to return to their
hometowns to be counted.
Joseph's family was from
Bethlehem, so Mary and
Joseph packed their bags
and joined the crowds
heading south.

There were so many people making the journey that
when they finally arrived, all the rooms in
all the inns were absolutely

full.

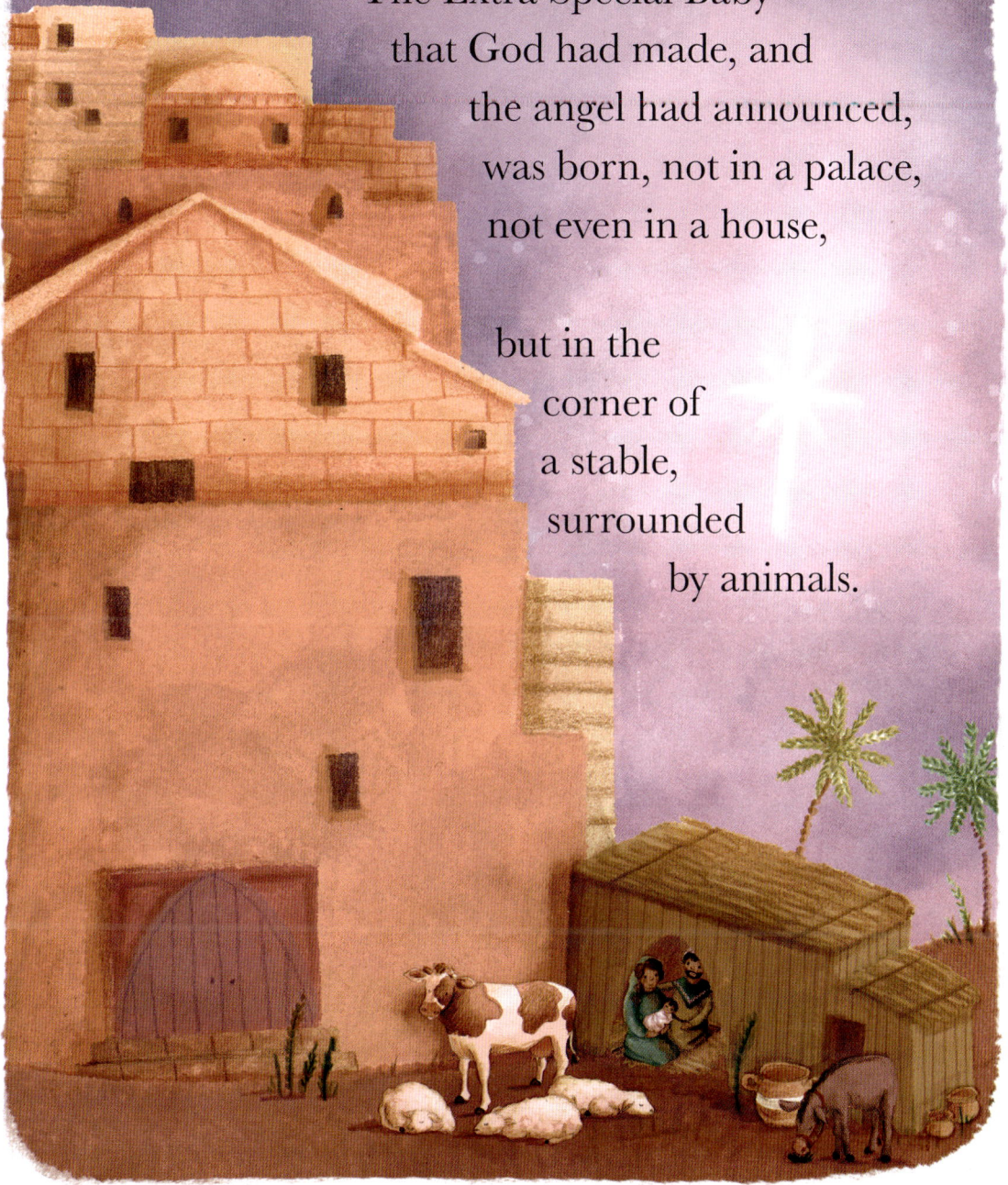

That night, Mary's baby was born.
The Extra Special Baby
that God had made, and
the angel had announced,
was born, not in a palace,
not even in a house,

but in the
corner of
a stable,
surrounded
by animals.

Outside Bethlehem, under the quiet night sky, some shepherds watched over their sheep.

Suddenly, an angel in glorious glow flooded the hillside with light.

"I have come to tell you some wonderful news. This very night, just over the hill, an **Extra Special Baby** has been born. He is the Son of God! You will find him in Bethlehem, lying in a manger full of straw."

All at once, the sky was full of light and colour and beautiful melodies, "Glory to God in heaven! Peace to his children on earth!"

The excited shepherds rushed over the hill into the town where they found the Extra Special Baby, Jesus, just as the angel had said.

Some time later, the long journey of the very clever men was almost at an end.

They had followed the star across hills and mountains, rivers and seas…

… until they finally reached Bethlehem.

"We discovered a Very Exciting Promise: the birth of the Extra Special One was written across time. We have come a long, long way to meet him."

And they laid out precious gifts
of shining gold,

sweet frankincense,
and
bitter myrrh.

That night, the angel came to Joseph again. "Pack your bags – it is no longer safe for you here. You must travel once more, this time to another land where the Extra Special Child can be out of harm's way."

So Mary, Joseph, and the young Jesus set off for a new home.

And in time…

… the extra
special
child grew…

… into an
extra special man,

who brought the blessings
of heaven to the people
of earth.

Stronger than a Storm

It was the end of a long and busy week.

Crowds of people had followed Jesus around, eager to be near him.

He had made sick people completely better; he had mended the legs of people who couldn't walk; and he had made the eyes of blind people see again.

Day after day, Jesus had shown the people astounding things right before their eyes,

as he told them how **much**

God

loved them.

Now Jesus and his twelve friends were ready for some peace and quiet as they stepped onto the waiting boat and set sail across the large lake.

Jesus was tired from a day of talking,
so he lay down to rest.

The gentle evening breeze soon turned into a blustery wind. It whipped the waves up into a great storm and soon the rocking boat was more than the men could manage.

"Jesus!" they shouted.
"Jesus, save us!
We're sinking!"

Jesus sat up, rubbed his eyes, and looked at them calmly.

"After everything you have seen and heard from me in the last few days, do you still not trust me to take care of you in a storm?"

Jesus stood up, looked straight out into the storm, and said,

"THAT'S ENOUGH!"

The rain
stopped.

The wind
ceased.

And the waves lapped gently against the boat
once more.

Jesus' friends were amazed.

"He can even make the weather better!" they said
to each other.

The Miraculous Meal

Crowds of people had flocked to hear Jesus and his friends teach them about God. Now they were a long way from home, the sun was setting, and lots of tummies were starting to

rumble.

One little boy opened his basket to eat, and as he did so, he overheard some grown-ups talking.

"Let's finish for the night. It's late, and we ought to tell everyone to go home and eat," they said.

The man in the middle smiled.

"They followed us here, so let's feed them," he said.

"How can we possibly feed them, Jesus?" asked one of his friends. "We haven't got any food, and even if we did, there must be

thousands

of hungry tummies out there!"

The little boy looked down at his basket. He had five loaves and two fish. Not much, but he had been taught it was kind to share.

He stood up.

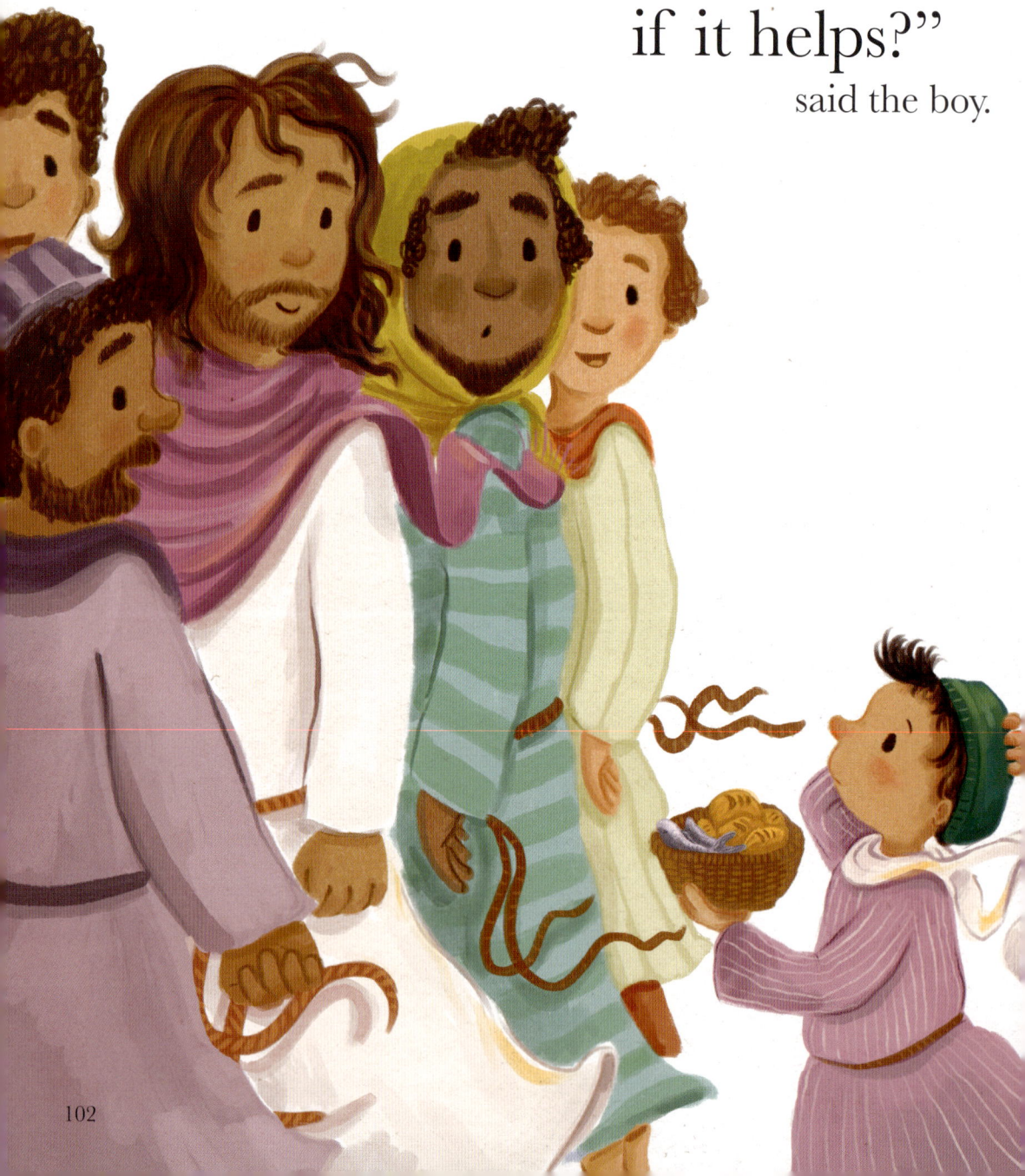

"Excuse me?
Erm, I've got a little bit of food in my basket,

if it helps?"

said the boy.

Jesus looked at him, smiled again,
and held out his hands. "Thank you," he said.

"And thank you Father God that you always
give us what we need." And he broke the bread
and fish into pieces and passed them around.

The food kept on coming!
There was more than enough for
everyone.

The Not-so-very-lost Lamb

There was a shepherd who owned a **hundred sheep** and he knew them all by name.

One day, a lovely butterfly
fluttered past and caught one
little lamb's attention.

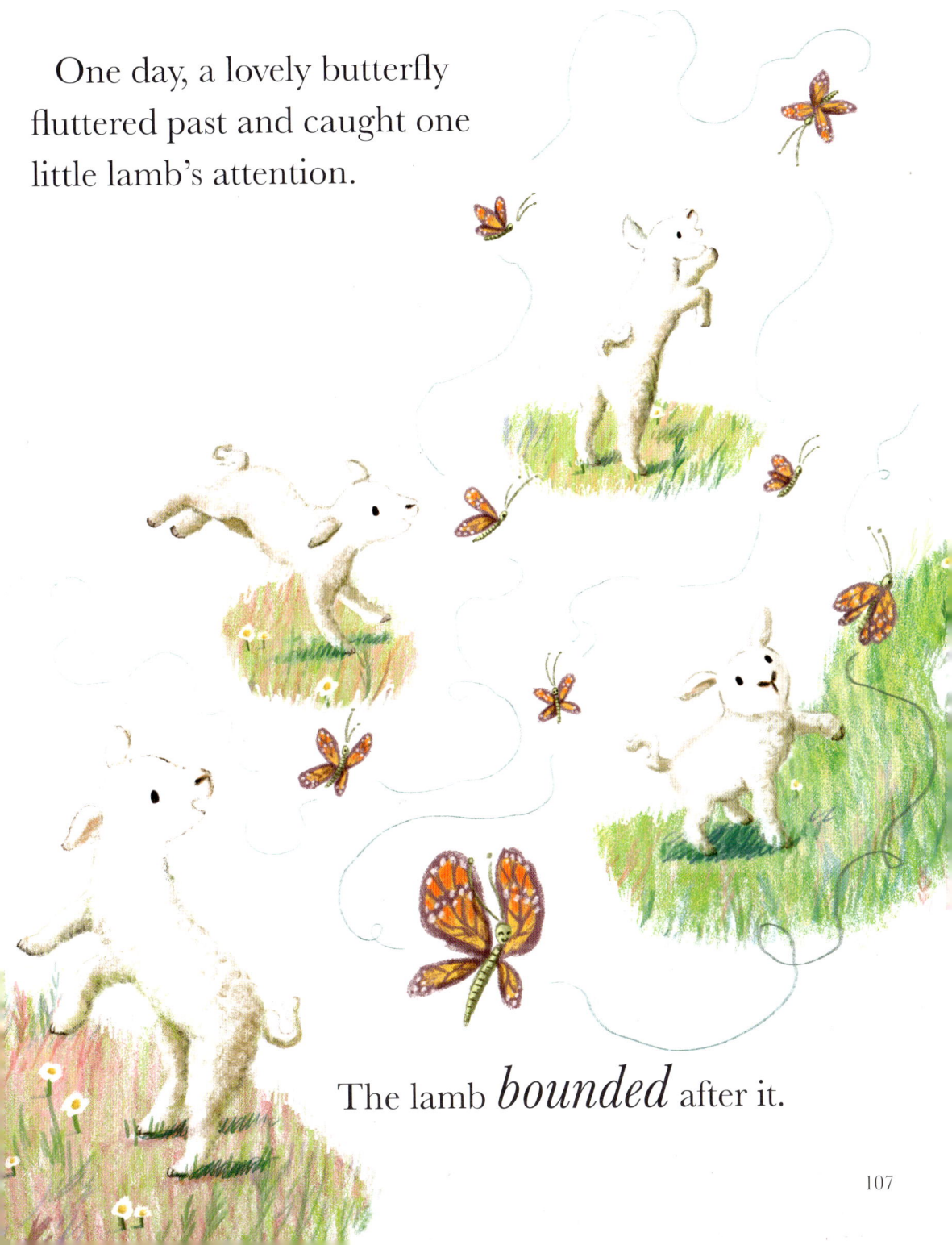

The lamb *bounded* after it.

Some bright flowers with a *delicious* scent
stopped the little lamb in its tracks.

"How delightful!"
thought the lamb.

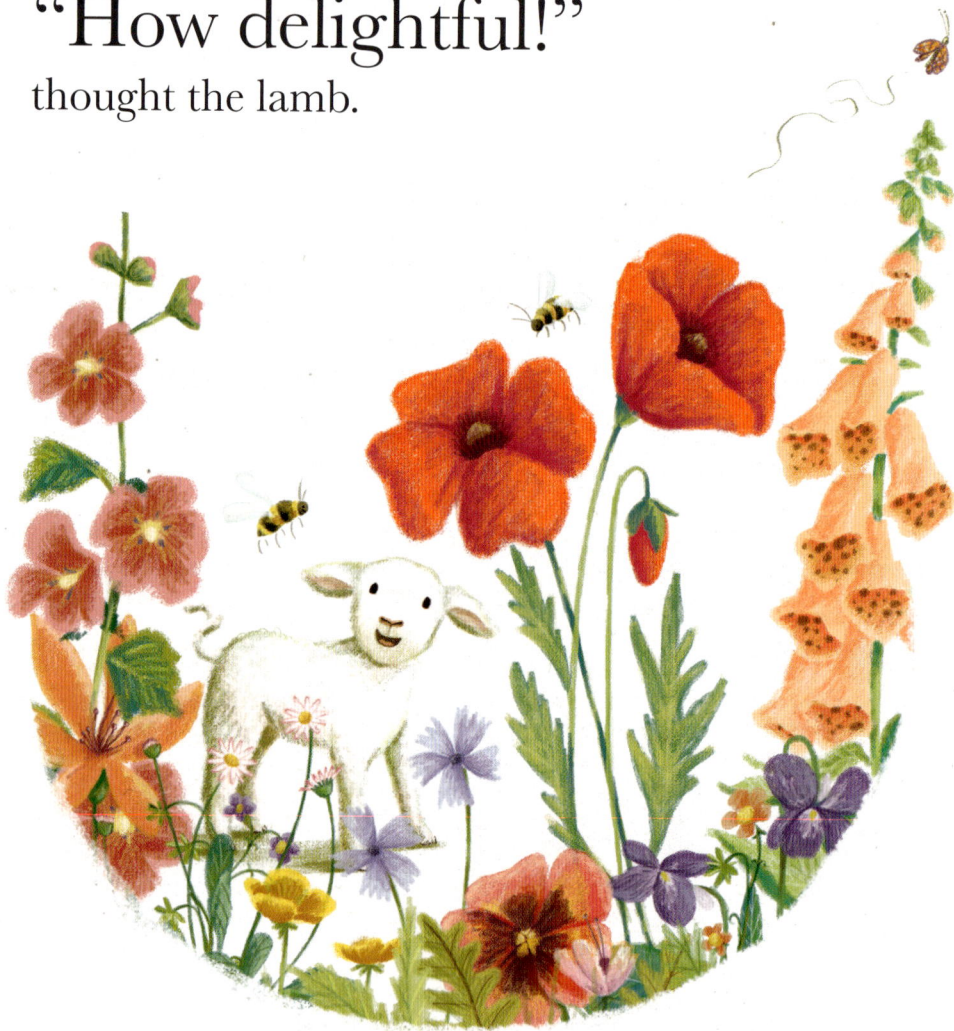

The little lamb came upon a meadow of lush,
green grass and a stream of sweet, clear water.

It ate and drank to its
heart's **content**.

A small herd of goats came *trotting* past and
the little lamb *frolicked* with the little goats.

It was a long and pleasant day, full of
wonder and surprise.

Though as the day wore on, the little lamb began to tire. It grew hungry again, but the grass here wasn't as *juicy* as it had been that morning.

The little lamb was thirsty, but the water was now dirty and bitter.

The butterfly was *nowhere* to be seen and the only flowers around had closed up for the night.
The little lamb looked for a friend to *play* with,
but the goats too had moved on.

It was growing rather DARK, and rather COLD, and the delights of the day seemed so *very* FAR away.

The little lamb looked up and realized it didn't know how far away it had wandered, or how to get *home.*

The little lamb felt very alone.

The shepherd had *ninety-nine* other sheep,
would he even notice ONE little lamb was missing?

As it stood there shivering,
it gave a small,
weak
bleat
of despair.

baaaa

At once, a beam of light shone around from beyond the trees.

A voice called,

"Little lamb?

Little lamb!"

The little lamb bleated again – louder, calling back,
"I'm here! Oh! I'm here!"
The little lamb was filled with such *joy*
and relief when it heard the sound
of the shepherd's voice.

"Oh, my lamb! As soon as I saw you were missing, I set out to find you, and I haven't *stopped* searching for you since!

You can *never* get so lost that I can't find you, and you can *never* wander so far away that you can't come back. My dear, precious lamb, you're safe, I'm here."

The Unexpected Friend

A man asked Jesus, "What must I do to live for ever in heaven with God?"

Jesus replied, "Tell me, what do you think?"

The man said,

"Well, I have been

taught that

I need to be friends

with God

and to

be kind

to his people.

But which

people

does he

mean?"

"I'll tell you a story," said Jesus,
"and maybe you can

work out

the answer."

An Israelite man was walking the long and rocky road from Jerusalem to Jericho.

Suddenly, a gang of robbers surrounded him and demanded that he give them all his money.

They pushed him around and grabbed everything that he had, even some of his clothes.

They were so **rough** that the man fell to the ground, bruised and hurting, as the robbers ran away.

Luckily, an important Israelite priest from the Temple was not far behind. He saw the man, and the man saw him, and hope rose in the man's heart; he thought help was on its way.

But the priest crossed to the other side of the road and hurried on by.
Perhaps he thought he was
too busy
to help.

Not long after, another man came along the road. He was called a Levite, someone who helped at the Temple. He saw the man, and the man saw him,

and once again hope rose in the man's heart.

Help was on its way.

But the Levite, possibly thinking the gang might still be around, hurried across to the other side of the road and **didn't look back.**

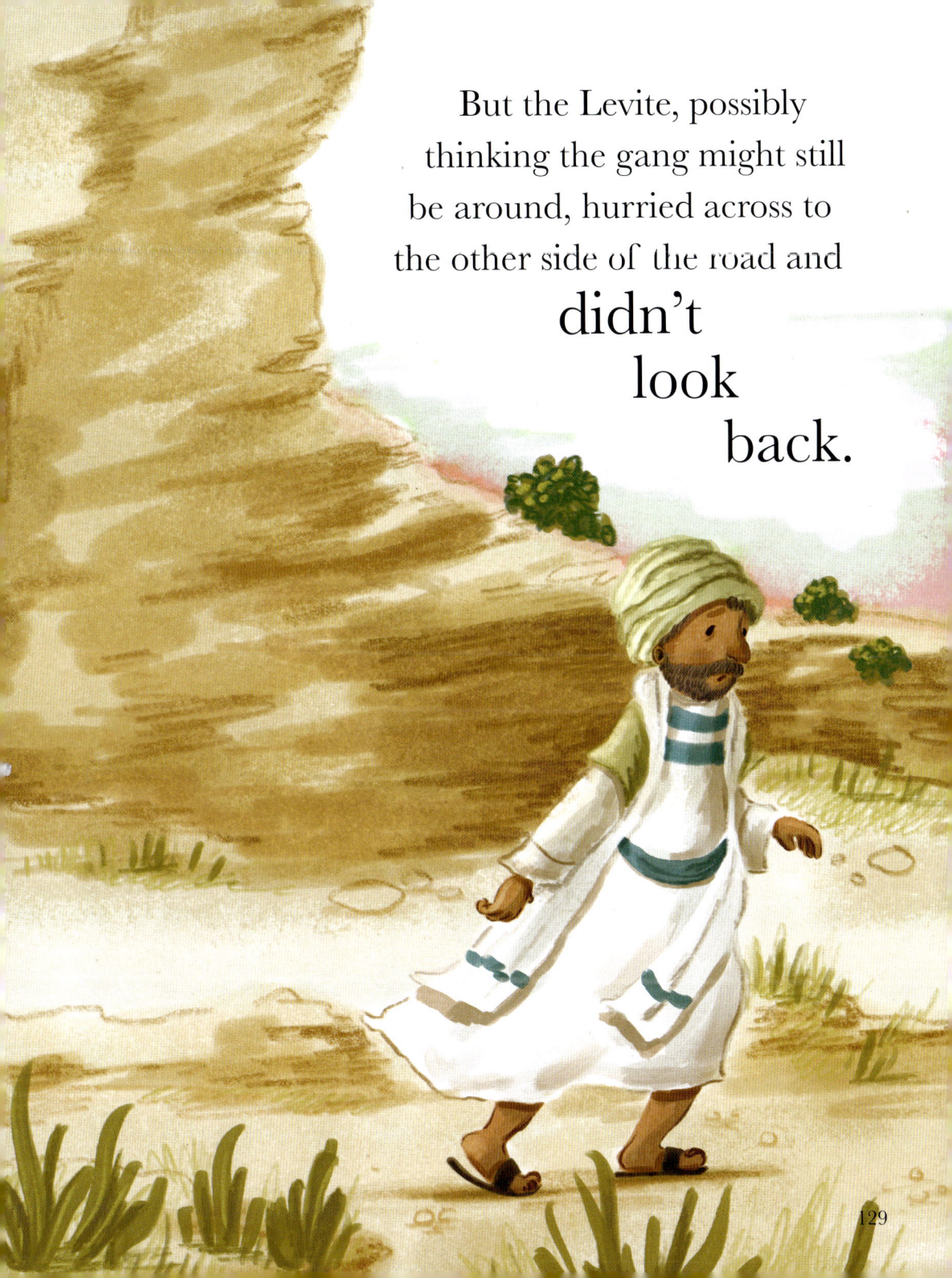

"If a priest and a Levite won't help me,"
thought the Israelite,

"who will?"

As the man lay there amongst the dirt and rubble,
he heard the sound of footsteps once again.

He opened his eyes, but seeing who it was,
he closed them again.

Who did the steps belong to?

"Not a Samaritan!" the man groaned.
"I don't want
any help from
him!"

Samaritans
don't
like
Israelites.

Israelites
don't
like
Samaritans.

But the steps got louder,
and nearer…

…and then they stopped.

The Samaritan knelt down
next to the Israelite.

He bandaged him up, and gently
lifted him onto his donkey.

He walked him carefully to the nearest inn and said,
"You can stay here until you are completely better.

I will pay whatever it costs."

"Which of the people in this story was kind?" asked Jesus.

"The Samaritan," said the man. "We don't have to be kind to them too, do we?"

"True **kindness** is for everyone," explained Jesus,

"even people you might not get along with.
That's **God's way!**"

The Promised One

Jesus was making a stir.
He made sick
people well.

He made food for thousands
out of almost nothing.

He cared for the lonely
and the needy.

He was like no one else,
and the people loved him.

At festival time, Jesus rode into the city of Jerusalem on a young donkey. As the crowds saw him coming, they welcomed him with shouts of joy.

"Here
comes
God-on-earth!"
they cheered.

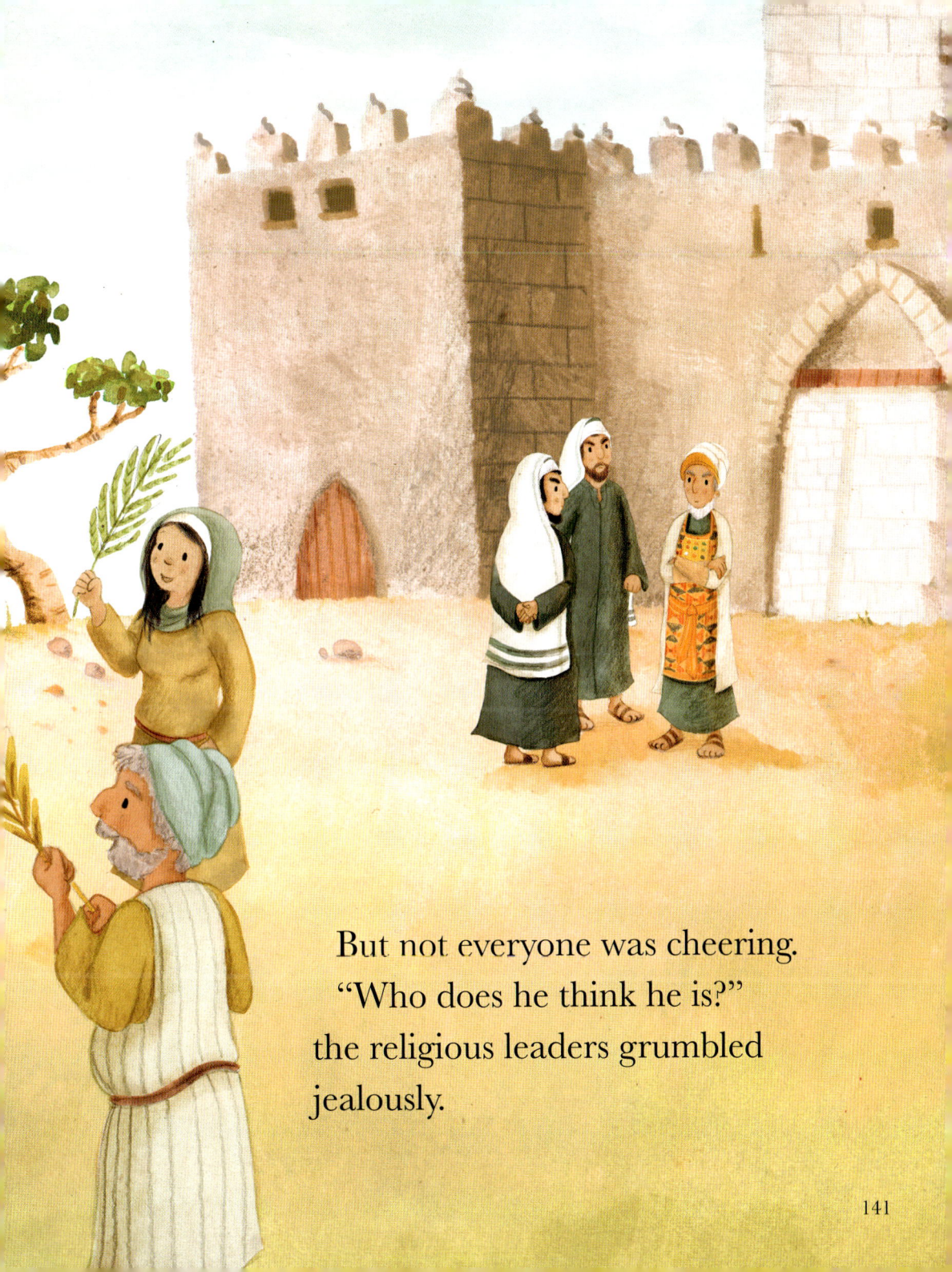

But not everyone was cheering.
"Who does he think he is?"
the religious leaders grumbled
jealously.

When Jesus saw the festival stalls at the Temple, he was frustrated.

"You should be here to meet with God, but you are only here to make money. How dare you turn this special place into an ordinary market!"

The religious leaders could stand it no longer.
Jesus was showing
them up!

He had to go.

Now, Jesus had twelve close friends who believed with all their hearts that he was God-on-earth, the Promised One

they had been

waiting for.

One evening, Jesus told them sadly, "The time is almost here when one of you will turn against me. But remember: these things are all part of God's plan. This bread and this wine are to remind you of my body and my blood.

When you meet together, think of me as you eat and drink them."

Jesus took three friends to a quiet garden to pray. "Father God, I know how terrible the next few days will be for me. If possible, please change this. But you always know best, so I will do whatever you ask."

The sound of footsteps and the light of torches interrupted the still darkness.

His close friend Judas was leading the way. Jesus knew they had come to arrest him.

All night long the religious leaders questioned
and accused Jesus.
"Are you the Promised One?
Do you really think you're
God-on-earth?"

Finally, they marched him to the local ruler, Pilate.
"This man is making trouble," they said.
"He claims to be the Son of God.
He must be silenced."

"Are you really God-on-earth?" Pilate asked.
But Jesus didn't say
                              a word.

"Take him away," Pilate said at last.

Jesus was led to a hill outside the city, where he was nailed to a **cross**.

Jesus' friends were devastated.

They thought Jesus was the Promised One.
They thought he was God-on-earth!

How could he let this happen?

But Jesus cried out with
a loud voice,
"My task is
complete!"

The earth rumbled loudly.
The sky went dark.

And Jesus died.

Two days later, Jesus' friends went to the tomb
where he had been laid.
But the heavy stone was rolled aside
and Jesus' body was
no longer there.

A shining *angel* was
waiting for them.

"You thought this was the end, but it's only the beginning," the angel said.

"God always has a plan: Jesus was dead… but he is **alive** again!"

In the days that followed, Jesus met with many
of his friends.
And he told them,
"You thought I had come for you,
in this place,
at this time.

But God's plans are bigger than you know!

I came for
everyone,
everywhere,

for all time."

Other gift books illustrated
by Antonia Woodward

The Lion Book of Nursery Prayers
Bedtime Prayers
Bible Promises for Baby's Christening
Bible Promises for Baby's Baptism
Bible Promises for Baby's Dedication
Our New Baby Memory Book